Verbs in Action
Move Along

Dana Meachen Rau

Marshall Cavendish
Benchmark
New York

2

Your friend moves the black checkers around the board. Now it is your turn to move. You jump over his checkers and take them off the board. Good move!

Your hands move when you wave. Your legs move when you jump.

Your arms and legs move when you swim. Your whole body moves when you dance.

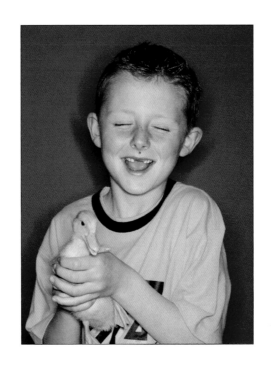

Even when you sit still, parts of you are moving. Your eyelids move up and down when you blink.

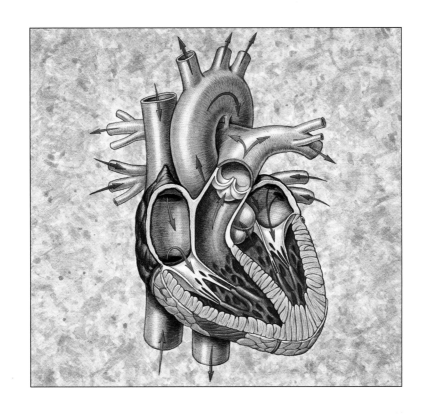

Inside your body, blood
moves through your *heart*.
Air moves through your *lungs*.

Animals move from place
to place in different ways.
Snakes *slither*. Rabbits jump.
Turtles crawl.

People and animals move
because they are alive.

Plants are alive, too. A flower may open in the day and close at night. It moves so slowly, you can hardly tell it is moving.

A swing moves back and forth.

A swing does not move by itself. It moves when someone pushes or pumps.

An elevator moves up and down.

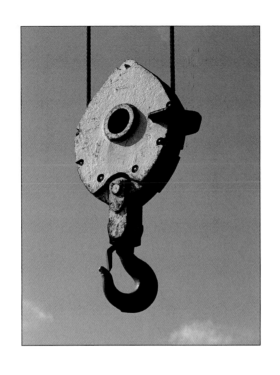

A wheel called a *pulley* helps the elevator move. A pulley and rope also lifts a curtain on a stage.

Objects keep moving until
something makes them stop.
This is called *inertia*. When a
ball rolls down a hill, it moves
very fast. The ground may slow
it down until it stops moving.

Or the ball might stop when it hits another object.

We cannot see some things that move. *Electricity* gives power to your television. Electricity moves through wires to make it work.

Sound moves through the air. When your friend hits a drum, the sound moves through the air to your ears. Your ears catch the *sound waves* and hear the beat.

Move can also mean to leave
one home to live in a new one.
When people move, they pack
up what they need in boxes.

Movers take the boxes and furniture from one place to another in a moving truck.

Your teacher might tell your class to "move along," if you are late for lunch.

At a museum, you might
"move on" to the next *exhibit*.

When you get in the car to go on a trip, you might say you are "on the move."

If you cry watching a sad movie, you might say it "moved" you.

Moving means that something or someone is in action.

At the park on a summer day, children play. Some slide. Some swing. Some jump rope and some seesaw. There is a lot of moving going on!

Challenge Words

electricity (ee-lek-TRIS-i-tee)—A type of power that makes machines run.

exhibit (eg-ZIB-it)—A display at a museum.

heart (HART)—The inside part of your body that pumps blood.

inertia (in-UR-shuh)—The movement of an object in a straight line until it is changed by another object or force.

lungs—The inside parts of your body that are used to breathe.

pulley (PULL-ee)—A wheel which has a rope or chain that moves around its edge.

slither (SLITH-uhr)—To slide and wiggle back and forth.

sound waves—Sound traveling through the air.

Index

Page numbers in **boldface** are illustrations.

With thanks to Nanci Vargus, Ed.D.
and Beth Walker Gambro, reading consultants

Marshall Cavendish Benchmark
Marshall Cavendish
99 White Plains Road
Tarrytown, New York 10591-9001
www.marshallcavendish.us

Library of Congress Cataloging-in-Publication Data

Rau, Dana Meachen, 1971-
Move along / by Dana Meachen Rau.
p. cm. — (Bookworms. Verbs in action)
Summary: "Discusses the action described by a verb, while making connections between people and
other living and nonliving objects. It also talks about other uses of the word in commonly used phrases."
—Provided by publisher.
Includes index.
ISBN-13: 978-0-7614-2291-4
ISBN-10: 0-7614-2291-9
1. Move (The English word)—Juvenile literature. 2. English
language—Verb—Juvenile literature. I. Title. II. Series.
PE1317.M68R38 2006
428.1—dc22
2005026781

Photo Research by Anne Burns Images

Cover Image by Corbis/Kevin. R. Morris

The photographs in this book are used with permission and through the courtesy of:
SuperStock: pp. 1, 12 Kwame Zikomo; p. 4 age fotostock; p. 6 Stockbyte; p. 16 Mauritius p. 17 Scott Barrow, Inc.;
p. 24 SuperStock; p. 26 Stock Image. *Corbis*: pp. 2, 23 Jon Feingersh; p. 5 Fabio Cardoso/zefa; p. 7 Images.com;
p. 8L Penny Tweedie; p. 8R D. Robert & Lorrie Franz; p. 9 Pat Doyle; p. 11 Darrell Gulin; p. 13 Simon Marcus;
p. 14 Gareth Brown; p. 15 Royalty Free; p. 18 Franco Vogt; p. 21 Tom Stewart; p. 22 Tom & Dee Ann McCarthy;
p. 25 Martin Rogers; p. 29 Tim Pannell.

Printed in Malaysia
1   3   5   6   4   2

Onondaga County Public Library
Syracuse, New York